An eye on
Women's Wellness

IGNITING THE FLAME OF FEMININE WELLNESS

INTRODUCTION

NURTURING WELL-BEING AT EVERY STAGE

Women's health is a multidimensional journey that spans various life stages, from adolescence through reproductive years to menopause and beyond. It's a holistic approach that acknowledges the physical, mental and emotional aspects of well-being.

MENSTRUAL HEALTH AND REPRODUCTIVE YEARS:

Women's health often begins with an understanding of menstrual health. This includes education on menstrual cycles, managing symptoms, and navigating reproductive health choices, such as family planning and fertility awareness.

MATERNAL HEALTH:

Pregnancy and childbirth represent transformative moments in a woman's life. Maternal health involves ensuring a healthy pregnancy, safe childbirth, and postpartum care for both mother and baby.

MENTAL AND EMOTIONAL WELL-BEING:

Women's mental health is a crucial aspect of overall wellness. This includes addressing stress, anxiety, and depression, as well as promoting self-care practices that contribute to emotional resilience.

PHYSICAL FITNESS AND NUTRITION:

Physical well-being for women involves tailored approaches to fitness and nutrition. Exercise routines, a balanced diet, and awareness of hormonal changes contribute to maintaining optimal health

HORMONAL HEALTH:

Understanding and managing hormonal changes, from puberty through menopause, is essential. This includes addressing issues like polycystic ovary syndrome (PCOS), menopausal symptoms, and hormonal imbalances.

SEXUAL AND REPRODUCTIVE RIGHTS:

Advocacy for sexual and reproductive rights is integral to women's health. Access to comprehensive healthcare, contraception, and family planning services empowers women to make informed choices about their bodies and lives.

DISEASE PREVENTION AND SCREENINGS:

Women-specific health screenings, such as mammograms and Pap smears, are vital for early detection of diseases. Breast health awareness and gynaecological check-ups play a crucial role in preventive care.

HOLISTIC WELLNESS:

Holistic wellness for women involves addressing the interconnectedness of physical, mental, and emotional health. Mind-body practices, stress management, and balancing work and life contribute to a fulfilling and healthy lifestyle.

Understanding and prioritizing women's health requires ongoing education, awareness, and advocacy. By embracing a comprehensive approach, we can empower women to proactively manage their well-being and lead healthy, vibrant lives.

MENSTRUAL HEALTH

MENSTRUAL CYCLE PHASES:

The menstrual cycle is divided into several phases, including menstruation, the follicular phase, ovulation, and the luteal phase. Each phase is regulated by hormonal changes that prepare the body for a potential pregnancy.

MENSTRUAL HYGIENE:

Maintaining good menstrual hygiene is essential. Using clean and appropriate menstrual products (like pads, tampons, or menstrual cups) and changing them regularly helps prevent infections and discomfort.

PAIN AND DISCOMFORT:

Many individuals experience symptoms such as cramps, bloating, and mood swings during menstruation. It's important to manage these symptoms through healthy lifestyle choices, proper nutrition, and, if necessary, with the help of medications.

IRREGULARITIES:

While some variation in the menstrual cycle is normal, persistent irregularities may indicate underlying health issues. Regular check-ups with a healthcare provider can help identify and address any concerns.

EMOTIONAL WELL-BEING:

Menstrual health is not just about physical well-being; it also includes emotional and mental health. Hormonal fluctuations during the menstrual cycle can affect mood and emotions. Taking care of one's mental health is crucial.

NUTRITION AND EXERCISE:

Maintaining a balanced diet and regular exercise can positively impact menstrual health. Adequate nutrition supports overall well-being, and regular exercise can help manage stress and reduce menstrual symptoms.

REPRODUCTIVE HEALTH:

Menstrual health is closely linked to reproductive health. Understanding one's menstrual cycle is essential for those trying to conceive or avoid pregnancy.

SEEKING PROFESSIONAL ADVICE:

If someone has concerns about their menstrual health, it's important to consult with a healthcare professional. They can provide personalized guidance, perform necessary tests, and address any underlying issues.

UNDERSTANDING MENSTRUAL CYCLES

The menstrual cycle is a complex, recurring process that the female body goes through each month, primarily in preparation for a potential pregnancy. Here's a simplified breakdown of the key phases:

MENSTRUATION (DAYS 1-5):

The cycle begins with menstruation, the shedding of the uterine lining. This results in the release of blood from the uterus through the vagina. Typically, this phase lasts about 3 to 7 days.

FOLLICULAR PHASE (DAYS 1-13):

This phase starts on the first day of menstruation and extends until ovulation. The pituitary gland releases follicle-stimulating hormone (FSH), stimulating the ovaries to produce several follicles, each containing an immature egg. One of these follicles will become dominant and continue to mature.

OVULATION (AROUND DAY 14):

Ovulation usually occurs around the middle of the menstrual cycle. The matured follicle releases an egg from the ovary into the fallopian tube. This is the most fertile period, and conception is most likely if sexual activity occurs around this time.

LUTEAL PHASE (DAYS 15-28):

After ovulation, the ruptured follicle transforms into a structure called the corpus luteum. This structure releases progesterone, which prepares the uterine lining for a potential pregnancy. If fertilization does not occur, the corpus luteum breaks down, and the cycle begins again with menstruation.

The menstrual cycle is regulated by hormones, primarily estrogen and progesterone, produced by the ovaries. The interaction of these hormones with the pituitary gland and the uterus orchestrates the various phases of the cycle.

It's important to note that the length of the menstrual cycle can vary from person to person, with an average cycle lasting around 28 days. Irregularities in the menstrual cycle can occur due to factors such as stress, changes in weight, hormonal imbalances, or underlying health conditions. Monitoring the menstrual cycle can be helpful for understanding fertility, planning or avoiding pregnancy, and identifying potential health concerns.

MANAGING MENSTRUAL SYMPTOMS

Menstrual symptoms can vary from person to person, but there are general strategies that can help manage them. Here are some tips:

HEALTHY DIET:
Maintain a balanced diet rich in fruits, vegetables, whole grains, and lean proteins. Limiting processed foods, caffeine, and sugary snacks may help regulate energy levels and reduce bloating.

HYDRATION:
Stay well-hydrated by drinking plenty of water. This can help alleviate bloating and may ease headaches associated with hormonal changes.

REGULAR EXERCISE:
Engage in regular physical activity. Exercise can help reduce menstrual pain and improve mood by releasing endorphins.

WARM COMPRESS:
Apply a warm compress to the lower abdomen to help relax muscles and alleviate cramps.

OVER-THE-COUNTER PAIN RELIEF:
Non-prescription pain relievers like ibuprofen or acetaminophen can help manage menstrual pain. Always follow the recommended dosage and consult with a healthcare provider if needed.

HERBAL TEAS:
Some herbal teas, such as ginger or peppermint, may have soothing effects and can help with bloating and discomfort.

HEALTHY SLEEP HABITS:
Ensure you get adequate sleep, as fatigue can exacerbate menstrual symptoms. Establish a consistent sleep routine and create a comfortable sleeping environment.

RELAXATION TECHNIQUES:

Practice relaxation techniques such as deep breathing, meditation, o
yoga to manage stress, which can impact menstrual symptoms.

STAY MINDFUL OF HORMONAL CHANGES:

Be mindful of hormonal changes throughout the menstrual cycle
Understanding your body's patterns can help you anticipate and manag
symptoms.

MAINTAIN A MENSTRUAL CALENDAR:

Track your menstrual cycle using a calendar or a mobile app. This ca
help you predict when your period is coming and prepare accordingly.

CONSIDER BIRTH CONTROL OPTIONS:

For some women, hormonal birth control methods, such as birt
control pills or hormonal IUDs, can help regulate menstrual cycles an
reduce symptoms.

TALK TO YOUR HEALTHCARE PROVIDER:

If menstrual symptoms are severe or significantly impacting you
quality of life, consult with your healthcare provider. They can provid
personalized advice and may suggest additional treatments o
medications.

HOT BATH OR SHOWER:

A warm bath or shower can help relax muscles and provide comfor
during menstruation.

ACUPRESSURE OR ACUPUNCTURE:

Some people find relief from menstrual symptoms throug
acupressure or acupuncture. Consult with a qualified practitioner t
explore these options.

MIND-BODY PRACTICES:

Mind-body practices like mindfulness meditation or biofeedbac
can help manage pain perception and improve overall well-being.

MENSTRUAL HYGIENE

Maintaining good menstrual hygiene is crucial for overall health and well-being. Here are some tips to ensure proper menstrual hygiene:

CHOOSE THE RIGHT MENSTRUAL PRODUCTS:

PADS:

Change disposable pads every 4-6 hours, or more often if needed. Choose pads with adequate absorbency for your flow.

TAMPONS:

Change tampons every 4-8 hours. Use the lowest absorbency needed and switch to a pad at night to reduce the risk of Toxic Shock Syndrome (TSS).

MENSTRUAL CUPS:

Empty and clean the cup every 8-12 hours. Follow the manufacturer's instructions for proper usage and cleaning.

WASH HANDS REGULARLY:

Always wash your hands before and after changing menstrual products to prevent the spread of bacteria.

KEEP EXTERNAL GENITAL AREA CLEAN:

During your period, clean the external genital area with mild, unscented soap and water. Avoid using harsh soaps or douches, as they can disrupt the natural balance of bacteria.

CHANGE REGULARLY:

Regularly change your menstrual products to prevent odor and reduce the risk of infection. This is especially important during heavy flow days.

PRACTICE PROPER DISPOSAL:

Dispose of used pads and tampons in designated bins. If using menstrual cups, empty the contents into the toilet and wash the cup before reinserting.

STAY HYDRATED:

Drink plenty of water during your period to stay hydrated. Proper hydration can help alleviate bloating and may contribute to overall well-being.

MANAGE ODOR:

Choose menstrual products with odor control, or consider using scented disposal bags for discreet and hygienic disposal.

BE MINDFUL OF CLOTHING:

Wear breathable, cotton underwear to allow proper airflow. Avoid tight-fitting clothes, as they can trap moisture and contribute to bacterial growth.

TRACK YOUR MENSTRUAL CYCLE:

Keep track of your menstrual cycle to anticipate your period's start date. This can help you be prepared and avoid any unexpected situations.

ADDRESS ANY CONCERNS PROMPTLY:

If you notice unusual symptoms, such as persistent itching, irritation or an unusual odor, consult with a healthcare professional for proper evaluation and guidance.

REPRODUCTIVE HEALTH

Reproductive health encompasses a broad range of topics related to the reproductive system, fertility, and overall well-being. Here are key aspects of reproductive health:

REGULAR CHECK-UPS:

Schedule regular visits with a healthcare provider for reproductive health exams and screenings. These may include pelvic exams, Pap smears, and breast exams.

CONTRACEPTION:

Explore and choose a contraceptive method that aligns with your reproductive goals. Options include birth control pills, condoms, intrauterine devices (IUDs), and more.

PRECONCEPTION CARE:

If planning to conceive, engage in preconception care. This involves adopting a healthy lifestyle, managing chronic conditions, and taking necessary supplements like folic acid.

SEXUAL HEALTH EDUCATION:

Stay informed about sexual health, including safe sex practices, sexually transmitted infection (STI) prevention, and understanding consent.

INFERTILITY AWARENESS:

If experiencing challenges with conception, consult with a fertility specialist. Infertility issues can have various causes, and there are often treatments available.

PREGNANCY AND PRENATAL CARE:

If pregnant, seek early prenatal care to monitor the health of both the mother and the developing fetus. This includes regular check-ups, screenings, and proper nutrition.

POSTPARTUM CARE:

After childbirth, prioritize postpartum care. This involves physica and emotional recovery, addressing any postpartum complications, anc seeking support when needed.

MENOPAUSE AND AGING:

Understand and manage the changes associated with menopaus and aging. This may include hormone replacement therapy, lifestyle adjustments, and regular health check-ups.

REPRODUCTIVE RIGHTS:

Advocate for and understand reproductive rights, including the right to access comprehensive reproductive healthcare, family planning services, and the ability to make informed choices about one's reproductive life.

EMOTIONAL WELL-BEING:

Recognize the emotional and mental aspects of reproductive health Seek support if dealing with issues such as fertility struggles, pregnancy loss, or postpartum depression.

SAFE ABORTION ACCESS:

Be aware of and advocate for access to safe and legal abortion service if needed. Reproductive rights include the right to make choices abou one's own body.

PREGNANCY

CONCEPTION:

It all starts with fertilization. When a sperm cell meets and penetrates an egg, fertilization occurs, forming a single-cell entity known as a zygote.

IMPLANTATION:

The zygote travels down the fallopian tube and into the uterus, where it embeds itself into the uterine lining. This is implantation, and it marks the beginning of pregnancy.

TRIMESTERS:

Pregnancy is divided into three trimesters, each lasting around three months. During these trimesters, the baby undergoes significant development, from a tiny cluster of cells to a fully formed fetus.

CHANGES IN THE MOTHER'S BODY:

Hormonal changes lead to various symptoms like morning sickness, fatigue, mood swings, and physical changes such as weight gain and breast enlargement.

CHILDBIRTH

LABOR:

The process begins with contractions that help the cervix dilate allowing the baby to move into the birth canal. This can take hours and is divided into early, active, and transitional phases.

DELIVERY:

This is the moment when the baby is born. The mother pushes during contractions, and with each push, the baby moves closer to being born. Once the baby's head and shoulders are out, the rest usually follow more easily.

PLACENTAL STAGE:

After the baby is born, the placenta, which provided nutrients to the baby during pregnancy, is expelled. This stage is often less dramatic than the actual delivery.

Throughout this process, healthcare professionals, such as midwives or doctors, monitor the mother and baby's well-being. Advances in medical science have provided various options for pain management during labor, and women may choose to give birth in hospitals, birthing centers, or at home, depending on their preferences and health considerations.

FERTILITY AWARENESS

Fertility awareness, or natural family planning, involves tracking and understanding a woman's menstrual cycle to determine the most fertile days for conception or, conversely, to identify the days when fertility is low to avoid pregnancy. It's a method that relies on observing and charting various signs and symptoms throughout the menstrual cycle.

Here are key aspects of fertility awareness:

MENSTRUAL CYCLE TRACKING:

Women typically ovulate (release an egg from the ovary) around the middle of their menstrual cycle. Tracking the menstrual cycle involves noting the start and end of each menstrual period.

BASAL BODY TEMPERATURE (BBT):

BBT is the body's resting temperature and tends to rise slightly after ovulation. By tracking this temperature daily, women can identify the shift that indicates ovulation has occurred.

CERVICAL MUCUS OBSERVATION:

The consistency and appearance of cervical mucus change throughout the menstrual cycle. Around ovulation, cervical mucus becomes clear, slippery, and stretchy, resembling egg whites.

CALENDAR METHOD:

This method involves keeping track of menstrual cycles over time to predict fertile days. It's based on the idea that ovulation usually occurs about 14 days before the start of the next menstrual period.

SYMPTOTHERMAL METHOD:

Combining various fertility signs, such as BBT, cervical mucus, and calendar tracking, to enhance the accuracy of predicting fertile and infertile days.

Fertility awareness can be used for both achieving and avoiding pregnancy, depending on the couple's goals. It requires consistent and accurate tracking, and it's most effective when couples have regular and predictable menstrual cycles. It's important to note that fertility

awareness does not protect against sexually transmitted infection
(STIs).

CONTRACEPTION OPTIONS

Certainly! There are various contraception options available, catering to different preferences, health considerations, and lifestyles. Here's an overview of some common methods:

HORMONAL METHODS:

BIRTH CONTROL PILLS:

Oral contraceptives that contain hormones (estrogen and/or progestin) to prevent ovulation and alter the cervical mucus.

PATCH:

A small adhesive patch worn on the skin that releases hormones to prevent pregnancy.

INJECTABLES:

Hormonal injections (usually progestin) administered every few months.

BARRIER METHODS:

CONDOMS:

Both male and female condoms provide a barrier to prevent sperm from reaching the egg. Male condoms are more widely used.

DIAPHRAGM:

A dome-shaped device inserted into the vagina to cover the cervix and block sperm.

INTRAUTERINE DEVICES (IUDS):

COPPER IUD:

Releases copper to prevent sperm from reaching the egg. It can stay in place for several years.

HORMONAL IUD:

Releases progestin to prevent ovulation and thicken cervical mucus, making it harder for sperm to reach the egg.

PERMANENT METHODS:

TUBAL LIGATION (FEMALE STERILIZATION):

A surgical procedure where the fallopian tubes are cut or blocked preventing eggs from reaching the uterus.

VASECTOMY (MALE STERILIZATION):
A surgical procedure that involves cutting or blocking the tubes that carry sperm.

EMERGENCY CONTRACEPTION:
MORNING-AFTER PILL:
A high dose of hormones taken after unprotected intercourse to prevent pregnancy. It's not intended for regular use.

NATURAL METHODS:
FERTILITY AWARENESS:
Tracking menstrual cycles, basal body temperature, and cervical mucus to identify fertile days and avoid unprotected intercourse during those times.

IMPLANTS:
BIRTH CONTROL IMPLANT:
A small rod inserted under the skin that releases hormones to prevent pregnancy for several years.

VAGINAL RING:
NUVARING:
A small, flexible ring inserted into the vagina that releases hormones to prevent pregnancy.

MENTAL HEALTH

Women's mental health encompasses a range of issues that can affect emotional and psychological well-being. Some common mental health concerns for women include:

DEPRESSION:
Women are more likely than men to experience depression. Hormonal factors, life events, and societal expectations can contribute to this.

ANXIETY DISORDERS:
Women also tend to be more prone to anxiety disorders, such as generalized anxiety disorder (GAD) and panic disorder.

EATING DISORDERS:
Conditions like anorexia nervosa, bulimia nervosa, and binge-eating disorder disproportionately affect women.

POSTPARTUM DEPRESSION:
After giving birth, some women may experience postpartum depression, which is characterized by feelings of sadness and despair.

MENOPAUSE AND MENTAL HEALTH:
Hormonal changes during menopause can impact mental health, leading to symptoms like mood swings and anxiety.

TRAUMA AND PTSD:
Women may be more likely to experience certain types of trauma, such as sexual assault or domestic violence, which can lead to post-traumatic stress disorder (PTSD).

CHRONIC STRESS:
The multiple roles women often juggle, such as caregiving, work, and family responsibilities, can contribute to chronic stress.

It's essential to approach women's mental health with sensitivity and awareness of the unique challenges they may face. Encouraging open conversations, reducing stigma, and promoting self-care and support networks are crucial steps in fostering positive mental health for women.

If you or someone you know is struggling, seeking professional help is always a good option.

STRESS MANAGEMENT

Stress management is crucial for women, considering the unique challenges they often face. Here are some stress management tips specifically tailored for women:

SELF-CARE RITUALS:

Prioritize self-care by incorporating regular self-care rituals into your routine. This could include activities like a warm bath, meditation, or simply taking time for yourself.

CONNECT WITH OTHERS:

Foster strong social connections. Talking to friends or joining support groups can provide emotional support and create a sense of community.

DELEGATE AND SHARE RESPONSIBILITIES:

Don't hesitate to delegate tasks at home or work. Share responsibilities with family members or colleagues to avoid feeling overwhelmed.

SET REALISTIC EXPECTATIONS:

Women often juggle multiple roles. Be realistic about what you can accomplish and set achievable goals. It's okay to ask for help when needed.

MIND-BODY EXERCISES:

Engage in mind-body exercises like yoga or tai chi. These practices not only promote physical health but also help in managing stress by combining movement with mindfulness.

JOURNALING:

Writing down your thoughts and feelings can be a therapeutic way to process stress. It can provide clarity and help you identify patterns or triggers.

LEARN TO SAY NO:

It's okay to decline additional commitments when you're already stretched thin. Learning to say no is a powerful way to manage stress and prioritize your well-being.

BALANCING HORMONES:
Recognize the impact of hormonal changes on stress levels. For example, practicing stress management techniques during menstruation, pregnancy, or menopause can be especially beneficial.

PROFESSIONAL SUPPORT:
If stress becomes overwhelming, consider seeking professional support. A therapist or counselor can provide guidance and coping strategies tailored to your unique circumstances.

TIME FOR CREATIVITY:
Engage in creative activities that bring you joy, whether it's painting, writing, or crafting. Creative expression can be a therapeutic outlet for stress.

Remember that self-care is not selfish; it's essential for overall well-being. Tailor these suggestions to fit your individual needs, and don't hesitate to seek support when needed.

ANXIETY AND DEPRESSION IN WOMEN

Anxiety and depression can affect anyone, but women may experience these conditions differently due to various factors, including hormonal fluctuations, societal expectations, and life experiences.

ANXIETY:
Generalized Anxiety Disorder (GAD): Women are more likely to be diagnosed with GAD, experiencing excessive worry and fear about various aspects of life.

PANIC DISORDER:
Women are also more prone to panic disorder, which involves sudden and intense episodes of fear, often accompanied by physical symptoms like rapid heartbeat and shortness of breath.

SOCIAL ANXIETY:

Some women may struggle with social anxiety, feeling intense self-consciousness and fear of judgment in social situations.

POST-TRAUMATIC STRESS DISORDER (PTSD):

Women are more likely to experience PTSD, often resulting from traumatic events such as sexual assault or domestic violence.

DEPRESSION:

Major Depressive Disorder (MDD): Women are diagnosed with depression at higher rates than men. Hormonal factors, life transitions, and societal pressures can contribute to this.

SEASONAL AFFECTIVE DISORDER (SAD):

Women may be more susceptible to SAD, a type of depression that occurs seasonally, often during the fall and winter months.

POSTPARTUM DEPRESSION (PPD):

After giving birth, some women experience postpartum depression, characterized by persistent feelings of sadness and hopelessness.

PREMENSTRUAL DYSPHORIC DISORDER (PMDD):

This severe form of premenstrual syndrome (PMS) can cause significant mood disturbances in the luteal phase of the menstrual cycle.

Addressing anxiety and depression in women involves a holistic approach:

PROFESSIONAL HELP:

Seek support from mental health professionals who can provide therapy, counseling, or medication when necessary.

SELF-CARE:

Prioritize self-care activities that promote mental well-being, such as exercise, adequate sleep, and relaxation techniques.

SOCIAL SUPPORT:

Build a strong support network of friends and family to share experiences and emotions.

COPING STRATEGIES:

Learn and practice coping strategies, such as mindfulness, cognitive-behavioural techniques, and stress management.

SELF-CARE PRACTICES

Self-care is essential for women to maintain physical, emotional, and mental well-being.

REGULAR EXERCISE:

Engage in physical activities that you enjoy, whether it's yoga, jogging, dancing, or any form of exercise. Regular movement is not only good for your physical health but also has positive effects on mood and stress levels.

ADEQUATE SLEEP:

Prioritize getting enough quality sleep. Establish a bedtime routine and create a sleep-conducive environment for a restful night.

MINDFULNESS AND MEDITATION:

Practice mindfulness and meditation to stay present in the moment and reduce stress. This can be especially beneficial for managing the various roles and responsibilities women often juggle.

HEALTHY NUTRITION:

Pay attention to your diet and ensure you're nourishing your body with a balanced and nutritious diet. Stay hydrated and make time for regular, nourishing meals.

PAMPERING YOURSELF:

Treat yourself to occasional pampering sessions, whether it's relaxing bath, a spa day, or simply taking time for skincare routines. It's great way to unwind and show yourself some love.

SET BOUNDARIES:

Learn to set healthy boundaries in both personal and professional relationships. Saying no when needed and prioritizing your own needs is crucial for maintaining balance.

CREATIVE OUTLETS:

Engage in creative activities that bring you joy, whether it's painting, writing, crafting, or any form of self-expression. Creative outlets can be therapeutic and provide a sense of fulfillment.

SOCIAL CONNECTION:

Nurture meaningful connections with friends and family. Spending time with loved ones can provide emotional support and a sense of community.

DIGITAL DETOX:

Take breaks from screens and social media. A digital detox can help reduce stress and promote a healthier relationship with technology.

EDUCATIONAL PURSUITS:

Invest time in activities that stimulate your mind and interests. Whether it's reading, taking a course, or learning a new skill, continuous learning can be fulfilling.

NATURE CONNECTION:

Spend time in nature. Whether it's a walk in the park, a hike, or simply sitting outdoors, connecting with nature has positive effects on mental well-being.

Remember that self-care is a personal journey, and it's important to tailor these practices to suit your individual needs and preferences. Regularly incorporating self-care into your routine can contribute to a healthier and more balanced lifestyle.

PHYSICAL WELL-BEING

Physical well-being is crucial for women to lead healthy and fulfilling lives. Here are some key aspects of physical well-being and tips for maintaining it:

REGULAR EXERCISE:

Engage in regular physical activity, such as cardiovascular exercises, strength training, and flexibility exercises. Find activities you enjoy to make exercise a sustainable part of your routine.

BALANCED NUTRITION:

Maintain a balanced and nutritious diet that includes a variety of fruits, vegetables, whole grains, lean proteins, and healthy fats. Stay hydrated by drinking an adequate amount of water.

REGULAR HEALTH CHECK-UPS:

Schedule regular check-ups and screenings to monitor your overall health. This includes mammograms, Pap smears, and other screenings recommended for your age and health status.

ADEQUATE SLEEP:

Prioritize getting enough quality sleep. Aim for 7-9 hours of sleep per night to support physical and mental well-being.

STRESS MANAGEMENT:

Practice stress management techniques, such as deep breathing, meditation, or yoga. Chronic stress can have adverse effects on both physical and mental health.

BONE HEALTH:

Ensure adequate intake of calcium and vitamin D for bone health. Weight-bearing exercises also contribute to maintaining strong and healthy bones.

REPRODUCTIVE HEALTH:

Attend regular gynecological check-ups and discussions about family planning, contraception, and menopause. Address any reproductive health concerns promptly.

HYGIENE PRACTICES:
Maintain good hygiene practices, including regular bathing, dental care, and skincare. This contributes to overall well-being and self-esteem.

HEART HEALTH:
Be mindful of heart health by adopting heart-healthy habits such as a nutritious diet, regular exercise, and avoiding smoking. Know your blood pressure and cholesterol levels.

POSTURE AND ERGONOMICS:
Pay attention to posture, especially if you have a sedentary job. Practice good ergonomics to prevent musculoskeletal issues and promote overall physical health.

BREAST HEALTH:
Conduct regular breast self-exams and be aware of any changes in your breast tissue. Report any concerns to your healthcare provider.

PREVENTIVE MEASURES:
Take preventive measures such as vaccinations and screenings for diseases like cervical cancer and breast cancer.

It's important for women to be proactive about their physical well-being and to seek medical advice and attention when needed. Regular self-care and healthy lifestyle choices contribute to a strong foundation for overall physical health.

EXERCISE ROUTINES FOR WOMEN

Creating a well-rounded exercise routine for women involves a combination of cardiovascular, strength training, flexibility, and balance exercises. Here's a suggested framework for a balanced exercise routine:

Cardiovascular Exercise (3-5 Times Per Week):

Option 1: 30 minutes of brisk walking, jogging, cycling, or swimming.

Option 2: High-intensity interval training (HIIT) for 20-30 minutes. This can include alternating between periods of intense exercise and short rest intervals.

Strength Training (2-3 Times Per Week):

Include exercises for major muscle groups: legs, arms, back, chest and core.

Examples: Squats, lunges, push-ups, bicep curls, tricep dips, and planks.

Use a combination of body weight, free weights, or resistance bands

Flexibility And Stretching (Daily Or At Least 3 Times Per Week):

Incorporate dynamic stretches before workouts and static stretches after workouts.

Include yoga or Pilates sessions for overall flexibility and balance.

Balance Exercises (2-3 Times Per Week):

Exercises like single-leg stands, heel-to-toe walk, or balancing on one foot can improve stability.

Yoga and Pilates also promote balance and body awareness.

Core Workouts (2-3 Times Per Week):

Include exercises targeting the abdominal muscles and lower back.

Examples: Planks, Russian twists, bicycle crunches, and leg raises.

REST AND RECOVERY:

Allow at least one or two days of rest per week to allow your body to recover.

Listen to your body and adjust intensity as needed to prevent overtraining.

NUTRITION AND DIET TIPS

Maintaining a balanced and nutritious diet is crucial for women's overall health and well-being. Here are some nutrition and diet tips:

BALANCED DIET:

Include a variety of foods from all food groups: fruits, vegetables, whole grains, lean proteins, and healthy fats.

Ensure a colourful plate with a mix of different-coloured fruits and vegetables to maximize nutrient intake.

ADEQUATE CALORIC INTAKE:

Consume an appropriate number of calories based on your age, activity level, and overall health goals.

PROTEIN INTAKE:

Include sources of lean protein such as poultry, fish, beans, lentils, tofu, and dairy products. Protein is essential for muscle health, especially if you're physically active.

CALCIUM AND VITAMIN D:

Ensure sufficient intake of calcium and vitamin D for bone health. Dairy products, fortified plant-based milk, leafy greens, and fatty fish are good sources.

IRON-RICH FOODS:

Include iron-rich foods like lean meats, beans, lentils, fortified cereals, and dark leafy greens to prevent iron deficiency.

FOLATE/FOLIC ACID:

If you're of childbearing age, ensure adequate folate intake to prevent neural tube defects during pregnancy. Sources include leafy greens, fortified cereals, and legumes.

HYDRATION:

Stay well-hydrated by drinking plenty of water throughout the day. Limit sugary beverages and excessive caffeine intake.

FIBER-RICH FOODS:

Include fiber-rich foods like whole grains, fruits, vegetables, and legumes to support digestive health and maintain a healthy weight.

HEALTHY FATS:

Choose sources of healthy fats such as avocados, nuts, seeds, and olive oil. Limit saturated and trans fats found in processed foods.

LIMIT ADDED SUGAR AND PROCESSED FOODS:

Minimize the intake of foods high in added sugars and processed foods. Opt for whole, unprocessed foods whenever possible.

MEAL TIMING:

Aim for regular meals and snacks to maintain consistent energy levels throughout the day.

LISTEN TO YOUR BODY:

Pay attention to hunger and fullness cues. Eat mindfully and avoid emotional eating.

LIMIT ALCOHOL INTAKE:

If you drink alcohol, do so in moderation. Limit the intake of alcoholic beverages and be mindful of their impact on overall health.

CONSIDER INDIVIDUAL NEEDS:

Individual nutritional needs vary, so consider consulting with a registered dietitian or healthcare professional to create a personalized nutrition plan.

MANAGING HORMONAL CHANGES

Managing hormonal changes is a crucial aspect of women's health especially during various life stages such as puberty, menstruation pregnancy, postpartum, perimenopause, and menopause. Here are some general tips for managing hormonal changes:

BALANCED DIET:

Maintain a well-balanced diet with a variety of nutrient-dense foods Include foods rich in calcium, iron, omega-3 fatty acids, and vitamins to support overall health.

REGULAR EXERCISE:

Engage in regular physical activity. Exercise can help regulate hormones, reduce stress, and contribute to overall well-being.

ADEQUATE SLEEP:

Prioritize sufficient and quality sleep. Sleep is crucial for hormonal balance and overall health.

STRESS MANAGEMENT:

Practice stress-reducing techniques such as deep breathing meditation, yoga, or mindfulness. Chronic stress can disrupt hormonal balance.

STAY HYDRATED:

Drink plenty of water to support overall health and maintain hydration.

LIMIT CAFFEINE AND ALCOHOL:

Limit the intake of caffeine and alcohol, as they can impact hormonal balance and disrupt sleep.

HEALTHY FATS:

Include sources of healthy fats in your diet, such as avocados, nuts seeds, and olive oil, which can support hormone production.

FIBER-RICH FOODS:

Incorporate fiber-rich foods like whole grains, fruits, vegetables, and egumes to support digestive health.

REGULAR HEALTH CHECK-UPS:
Attend regular check-ups with your healthcare provider to monitor ormonal levels and address any concerns.

HORMONE REPLACEMENT THERAPY (HRT):
For women experiencing severe symptoms during menopause, ormone replacement therapy may be considered under the guidance of healthcare professional.

BIRTH CONTROL METHODS:
If using hormonal contraceptives, discuss options with your ealthcare provider to find the most suitable method for your needs.

MIND-BODY PRACTICES:
Practices such as yoga and meditation can help manage stress and romote hormonal balance.

SUPPLEMENTS:
Consider supplements like calcium, vitamin D, and omega-3 fatty cids, especially if dietary intake is insufficient. However, consult with a ealthcare professional before starting any supplements.

COMMUNITY AND SUPPORT:
Connect with others who may be going through similar experiences. haring experiences and seeking support can be beneficial.

EDUCATE YOURSELF:
Understand the hormonal changes specific to your life stage. Knowledge empowers you to make informed decisions and manage ymptoms effectively.

HORMONAL HEALTH

Women's hormonal health is a complex and dynamic aspect of overal well-being. Hormones play a crucial role in various physiologica processes throughout a woman's life.

PUBERTY:

ESTROGEN AND PROGESTERONE:

These hormones regulate the development of secondary sexua characteristics, menstrual cycles, and reproductive organs.

MENSTRUAL CYCLE:

FOLLICLE-STIMULATING HORMONE (FSH):

Stimulates the growth of ovarian follicles.

LUTEINIZING HORMONE (LH):

Triggers ovulation.

ESTROGEN AND PROGESTERONE:

Fluctuate throughout the menstrual cycle, influencing the menstrua cycle phases.

PREGNANCY:

HUMAN CHORIONIC GONADOTROPIN (HCG):

Maintains the corpus luteum during early pregnancy.

ESTROGEN AND PROGESTERONE:

Support pregnancy and fetal development.

POSTPARTUM:

PROLACTIN:

Stimulates milk production for breastfeeding.

OXYTOCIN:

Promotes uterine contractions during labor and stimulates mil ejection during breastfeeding.

PERIMENOPAUSE:

Fluctuations in Estrogen and Progesterone: Irregular menstrua cycles and symptoms like hot flashes and mood swings may occur.

MENOPAUSE:

Decrease in Estrogen and Progesterone: Leads to the end of menstrual cycles and various symptoms such as hot flashes, night sweats, and changes in bone density.

Maintaining hormonal balance is essential for women's health. Here are some general tips to support hormonal health:

BALANCED DIET:

Consume a nutrient-rich diet with a variety of fruits, vegetables, whole grains, lean proteins, and healthy fats to support hormonal production.

REGULAR EXERCISE:

Engage in regular physical activity to regulate hormones, manage stress, and support overall well-being.

ADEQUATE SLEEP:

Prioritize sufficient and quality sleep for hormonal balance and overall health.

STRESS MANAGEMENT:

Practice stress-reducing techniques such as meditation, deep breathing, or yoga to mitigate the impact of chronic stress on hormonal health.

REGULAR HEALTH CHECK-UPS:

Attend regular check-ups with your healthcare provider to monitor hormonal levels and address any concerns.

HORMONE REPLACEMENT THERAPY (HRT):

For women experiencing severe symptoms during menopause, HRT may be considered under the guidance of a healthcare professional.

MENOPAUSE AND PERIMENOPAUSE

Menopause and perimenopause are natural phases in a woman's life associated with hormonal changes. Here's an overview of both:

PERIMENOPAUSE:

Definition: Perimenopause is the transitional phase leading up to menopause. It typically begins in the 40s but can start earlier or later.

Duration: It can last for several years, and during this time, hormonal fluctuations become more pronounced.

Hormonal Changes: Estrogen and progesterone levels fluctuate, and women may experience irregular menstrual cycles, hot flashes, night sweats, mood swings, and changes in libido.

Symptoms: Symptoms can vary widely among women, and not everyone experiences the same intensity or combination of symptoms.

Fertility: Fertility declines during perimenopause, and women may still become pregnant but with increased difficulty.

MENOPAUSE:

Definition: Menopause is the point when a woman has not had a menstrual period for 12 consecutive months, marking the end of her reproductive years.

Average Age: The average age of natural menopause is around 51, but it can occur earlier or later.

Hormonal Changes: Estrogen and progesterone levels significantly decrease, leading to the cessation of menstrual cycles.

Symptoms: Common symptoms include hot flashes, night sweats, sleep disturbances, mood changes, vaginal dryness, and changes in bone density.

HEALTH CONSIDERATIONS:

The decline in estrogen levels can impact bone health, cardiovascular health, and may increase the risk of osteoporosis and heart disease.

MANAGEMENT:

Hormone Replacement Therapy (HRT) may be considered for managing severe symptoms, but it involves risks and benefits that should be discussed with a healthcare professional.

Tips for Managing Perimenopause and Menopause:

HEALTHY LIFESTYLE:

Adopt a healthy diet rich in calcium and vitamin D for bone health. Engage in regular exercise to support overall well-being.

MIND-BODY PRACTICES:

Practice stress-reducing techniques such as meditation, yoga, or deep breathing.

STAY CONNECTED:

Seek support from friends, family, or support groups to share experiences and coping strategies.

HORMONE REPLACEMENT THERAPY (HRT):

Discuss the potential benefits and risks of HRT with a healthcare professional to make an informed decision.

REGULAR CHECK-UPS:

Attend regular health check-ups to monitor bone density, cardiovascular health, and overall well-being.

It's important to approach perimenopause and menopause as natural phases of life and to prioritize self-care during these transitions. Seeking guidance from healthcare professionals can help manage symptoms and ensure optimal health during this time.

HORMONAL IMBALANCES

Hormonal imbalances in women can occur at various stages in life and may lead to a range of symptoms.

POLYCYSTIC OVARY SYNDROME (PCOS):

Hormones Affected: Insulin, androgens (e.g., testosterone luteinizing hormone (LH), and follicle-stimulating hormone (FSH).

Symptoms: Irregular menstrual cycles, cysts on the ovaries, acne excessive facial and body hair, and fertility issues.

THYROID DISORDERS:

Hormones Affected: Thyroid hormones (T3 and T4 thyroid-stimulating hormone (TSH).

Symptoms: Hypothyroidism (underactive thyroid) can caus fatigue, weight gain, and depression. Hyperthyroidism (overactiv thyroid) can lead to weight loss, anxiety, and increased heart rate.

ESTROGEN DOMINANCE:

Hormones Affected: Imbalance between estrogen an progesterone.

Symptoms: Heavy or irregular periods, breast tenderness, moo swings, and sleep disturbances.

ADRENAL FATIGUE:

Hormones Affected: Cortisol (stress hormone), DHEA.

Symptoms: Fatigue, difficulty handling stress, changes in mood, an disrupted sleep patterns.

PREMENSTRUAL SYNDROME (PMS):

Hormones Affected: Fluctuations in estrogen and progesterone.

Symptoms: Mood swings, irritability, bloating, breast tendernes and changes in appetite before menstruation.

MENOPAUSE:

Hormones Affected: Decline in estrogen and progesterone.

Symptoms: Hot flashes, night sweats, mood swings, vaginal drynes and changes in bone density.

HYPERPROLACTINEMIA:

Hormones Affected: Prolactin (responsible for milk production).
Symptoms: Irregular menstrual cycles, breast discharge, and infertility.

MANAGING HORMONAL IMBALANCES:

CONSULT A HEALTHCARE PROFESSIONAL:

If you suspect a hormonal imbalance, consult with a healthcare professional for proper diagnosis and guidance.

HEALTHY LIFESTYLE:

Maintain a balanced diet, engage in regular exercise, and prioritize sufficient sleep.

STRESS MANAGEMENT:

Practice stress-reducing techniques such as meditation, deep breathing, or yoga.

HORMONE REPLACEMENT THERAPY (HRT):

For certain conditions, hormone replacement therapy may be recommended under the guidance of a healthcare professional.

MEDICATION:

Some hormonal imbalances may be managed with medications prescribed by a healthcare provider.

REGULAR CHECK-UPS:

Attend regular check-ups to monitor hormonal levels and overall health.

It's essential to approach hormonal imbalances with a comprehensive and individualized strategy. Working closely with healthcare professionals can help identify the underlying causes and develop an appropriate treatment plan.

THYROID HEALTH

Thyroid health is crucial for overall well-being, and women are more prone to thyroid disorders than men. The thyroid gland produces hormones that play a vital role in regulating metabolism, energy levels, and various bodily functions. Here are key aspects of thyroid health in women:

COMMON THYROID DISORDERS:
HYPOTHYROIDISM:
An underactive thyroid, where the gland doesn't produce enough thyroid hormones (T3 and T4).

HYPERTHYROIDISM:
An overactive thyroid, leading to excessive production of thyroid hormones.

SYMPTOMS OF THYROID DISORDERS:
Hypothyroidism Symptoms: Fatigue, weight gain, cold intolerance, dry skin, and depression.

Hyperthyroidism Symptoms: Weight loss, increased heart rate, heat intolerance, anxiety, and tremors.

CAUSES OF THYROID DISORDERS:
Autoimmune Conditions: Hashimoto's thyroiditis (hypothyroidism) and Graves' disease (hyperthyroidism) are autoimmune conditions affecting the thyroid.

Iodine Deficiency Or Excess: An imbalance in iodine levels can impact thyroid function.

Genetics: Thyroid disorders can run in families.

THYROID HEALTH DURING PREGNANCY:
Importance Of Iodine: Iodine is crucial during pregnancy for the development of the baby's brain and thyroid gland.

Monitoring Thyroid Levels: Pregnant women with thyroid disorders may need careful monitoring and adjustment of medication.

THYROID CANCER:

Risk Factors: Women are more likely to develop thyroid cancer. Regular check-ups and early detection are essential.

MANAGING THYROID HEALTH:

Regular Check-Ups: Routine thyroid function tests can help detect and manage thyroid disorders.

Balanced Diet: Ensure sufficient iodine intake through a balanced diet, including iodized salt and seafood.

Medication: Thyroid hormone replacement (for hypothyroidism) or anti-thyroid medications (for hyperthyroidism) may be prescribed.

Stress Management: Chronic stress can impact thyroid health, so stress-reducing techniques are beneficial.

THYROID SCREENING:

Age-Specific Guidelines: Regular thyroid screening is advisable, especially for women over the age of 35 or those with risk factors.

Symptoms Or Pregnancy: If experiencing symptoms or during pregnancy, thyroid screening may be more frequent.

IODINE SUPPLEMENTATION:

Consultation With Healthcare Provider: If considering iodine supplements, consult with a healthcare provider. Excessive iodine intake can also have negative effects.

SEXUAL HEALTH

Sexual health is an integral aspect of overall well-being for women. I encompasses physical, emotional, and mental well-being related to sexua experiences and relationships.

COMMUNICATION:

Open and honest communication with partners about desires boundaries, and concerns is crucial for a healthy sexual relationship.

CONSENT:

Ensuring mutual consent is fundamental in any sexual relationship Both partners should feel comfortable and willing to engage in sexua activities.

SAFE SEX PRACTICES:

Using protection, such as condoms, is important for preventin; sexually transmitted infections (STIs) and unintended pregnancies.

REGULAR GYNECOLOGICAL CHECK-UPS:

Regular visits to a healthcare provider for gynaecological check-ups screenings, and discussions about sexual health are essential.

MENSTRUAL HEALTH:

Understanding one's menstrual cycle, managing menstrua symptoms, and addressing any irregularities contribute to overall sexua well-being.

PELVIC HEALTH:

Pelvic health is crucial for sexual function. Pelvic floor exercises and seeking professional help for pelvic health concerns can be beneficial.

HORMONAL CHANGES:

Being aware of how hormonal changes, such as those durin; menstruation, pregnancy, and menopause, can affect sexual health and intimacy.

SEXUAL DESIRE AND SATISFACTION:

Sexual desire and satisfaction vary among individuals. It's normal fo these aspects to change over time and in response to life events.

EMOTIONAL WELL-BEING:
Emotional well-being plays a significant role in sexual health. Addressing stress, anxiety, and relationship issues can positively impact sexual experiences.

VAGINAL HEALTH:
Maintaining good vaginal hygiene, addressing infections promptly, and using appropriate lubrication can contribute to vaginal health.

SEXUAL EDUCATION:
Ongoing sexual education helps individuals make informed decisions about their sexual health. This includes knowledge about contraception, STIs, and reproductive health.

MENTAL HEALTH:
Mental health is interconnected with sexual health. Conditions such as depression or anxiety can affect libido and sexual satisfaction.

LIFESTYLE FACTORS:
Adopting a healthy lifestyle, including regular exercise, a balanced diet, and sufficient sleep, positively influences sexual health.

PELVIC PAIN AND SEXUAL DYSFUNCTION:
Seeking professional help for pelvic pain or sexual dysfunction is important. These issues can have physical and psychological components.

SEEKING HELP:
If experiencing challenges or concerns related to sexual health, seeking guidance from a healthcare professional or a qualified therapist can be beneficial.

SEXUAL EDUCATION FOR WOMEN

Absolutely, let's dive in! Sexual education for women encompasses various aspects to foster a comprehensive understanding of their bodies, relationships, and sexual health. Here are some key components:

ANATOMY AND REPRODUCTIVE HEALTH:

Understanding the female reproductive system, including the menstrual cycle, ovulation, and menstruation. Learning about different parts of the female anatomy, like the vulva, vagina, uterus, and ovaries.

CONTRACEPTION:

Exploring different methods of birth control and their effectiveness.

Understanding how to make informed decisions about contraception based on individual needs and circumstances.

SEXUALLY TRANSMITTED INFECTIONS (STIS):

Awareness of common STIs, their symptoms, prevention, and testing.

Promoting safe sexual practices to reduce the risk of STIs.

RELATIONSHIPS AND COMMUNICATION:

Emphasizing the importance of open communication in relationships, including consent and boundaries.

Recognizing healthy and respectful relationships.

EMOTIONAL WELL-BEING:

Addressing the emotional aspects of sexual health, including self-esteem, body image, and mental well-being.

PLEASURE AND SEXUAL SATISFACTION:

Acknowledging the importance of sexual pleasure and satisfaction in a consensual and respectful context.

Encouraging a positive attitude towards one's own body and sexual experiences.

REPRODUCTIVE CHOICES:

Providing information about reproductive choices, including family planning, pregnancy, and childbirth.

CULTURAL AND SOCIAL CONTEXT:

Recognizing and respecting diverse cultural perspectives on sexuality.

Addressing societal norms and expectations related to women's sexuality.

ONLINE AND DIGITAL SAFETY:

Navigating the digital landscape responsibly, understanding online risks, and practicing digital safety in the context of relationships.

REGULAR HEALTH CHECK-UPS:

Encouraging regular gynecological check-ups and screenings for early detection of any health concerns.

Sexual education empowers women to make informed choices, prioritize their well-being, and navigate their sexual journey with confidence and respect. If you have specific questions or want more details on any of these points, feel free to ask!

INTIMACY AND RELATIONSHIPS

Intimacy and relationships are complex and beautiful aspects of life, and women experience them in diverse and unique ways. Here are some key considerations when it comes to intimacy and relationships for women:

EMOTIONAL CONNECTION:

Many women value emotional intimacy as a crucial aspect of a relationship. This involves sharing feelings, thoughts, and experiences with a partner.

COMMUNICATION:

Effective communication is the foundation of any healthy relationship. Women often appreciate open and honest conversations, where they feel heard and understood.

RESPECT AND EQUALITY:

Mutual respect and equality are essential. Women, like anyone else, want to be treated with respect and as equal partners in a relationship.

BOUNDARIES:

Establishing and respecting boundaries is crucial. Women, like everyone, have individual comfort levels and limits that should be acknowledged and honored.

PHYSICAL INTIMACY:

Physical intimacy can be important, but it varies from person to person. Some women may prioritize physical closeness, while others may emphasize other forms of connection.

TRUST:

Building and maintaining trust is key. Trust forms the foundation of a strong and healthy relationship, and women often value partners who are reliable and trustworthy.

SUPPORT:

Women may seek emotional support from their partners during challenging times. Being there for each other in both good and difficult moments fosters a deeper connection.

SHARED VALUES AND GOALS:

Having shared values and goals can strengthen a relationship. Women often appreciate partners who share common interests and long-term objectives.

INDEPENDENCE:

Maintaining individual identities and personal growth is essential. Women, like anyone else, value partners who support their ambitions and encourage personal development.

CULTURAL AND SOCIAL CONTEXT:

Recognizing and respecting cultural and social influences on relationships is important. Expectations and norms can vary, and understanding these dynamics can contribute to a healthier connection.

Remember, these are general considerations, and every woman is unique in her preferences and experiences. It's crucial to communicate openly with a partner, be attentive to each other's needs, and work together to build a relationship that feels fulfilling for both parties. If you have specific questions or want to explore any aspect further, feel free to ask!

COMMON SEXUAL HEALTH ISSUES

Women may encounter various sexual health issues throughout their lives. Here are some common concerns:

MENSTRUAL DISORDERS:

Conditions like irregular periods, heavy bleeding (menorrhagia), or absence of menstruation (amenorrhea) can affect sexual health.

SEXUALLY TRANSMITTED INFECTIONS (STIS):

Infections such as chlamydia, gonorrhea, herpes, and HPV can impact women's sexual health. Regular testing and safe sexual practices are essential.

VAGINAL INFECTIONS:

Yeast infections and bacterial vaginosis are common and can cause discomfort and affect sexual well-being.

ENDOMETRIOSIS:

Endometriosis is a condition where tissue similar to the lining of the uterus grows outside the uterus. It can cause pain during intercourse and affect fertility.

PELVIC INFLAMMATORY DISEASE (PID):

PID is an infection of the reproductive organs that can lead to pelvic pain and potentially impact fertility.

SEXUAL DYSFUNCTION:

Conditions like low libido, arousal disorders, and pain during intercourse (dyspareunia) can affect sexual satisfaction.

POLYCYSTIC OVARY SYNDROME (PCOS):

PCOS can cause hormonal imbalances, irregular periods, and may impact fertility.

URINARY TRACT INFECTIONS (UTIS):

UTIs can cause discomfort during sex and may lead to other complications if left untreated.

MENOPAUSE-RELATED CHANGES:

Hormonal changes during menopause can result in vaginal dryness, decreased libido, and changes in sexual function.

PELVIC FLOOR DISORDERS:

Issues such as pelvic organ prolapse or incontinence can impact sexual health and overall well-being.

It's important for women to prioritize their sexual health by seeking regular check-ups, communicating openly with healthcare providers, practicing safe sex, and addressing any concerns promptly. If you have specific questions about any of these issues or want more information, feel free to ask!

DISEASE PREVENTION

Preventive measures play a crucial role in maintaining women's health
Here are some key aspects of disease prevention for women:

REGULAR HEALTH CHECK-UPS:

Schedule regular check-ups with a healthcare provider fc
screenings, vaccinations, and overall health assessments.

BREAST HEALTH:

Perform regular breast self-exams and, depending on age and ris
factors, undergo mammograms as recommended by healthcar
professionals.

CERVICAL CANCER SCREENING:

Regular Pap smears or HPV tests help detect cervical abnormaliti
early, reducing the risk of cervical cancer.

IMMUNIZATIONS:

Stay up-to-date on vaccinations, including those for HPV, flu, an
other preventable diseases.

HEART HEALTH:

Adopt a heart-healthy lifestyle with regular exercise, a balanced die
and maintaining a healthy weight to reduce the risk of cardiovascula
diseases.

BONE HEALTH:

Ensure an adequate intake of calcium and vitamin D for stron
bones. Weight-bearing exercises also contribute to bone health.

SEXUAL HEALTH:

Practice safe sex to prevent sexually transmitted infections (STIs
Regular screenings for STIs are essential, especially if sexually active wit
new or multiple partners.

HEALTHY LIFESTYLE CHOICES:

Adopt a healthy lifestyle that includes a balanced diet, regula
exercise, sufficient sleep, and stress management.

MENTAL HEALTH:

Prioritize mental well-being by seeking support when needed, managing stress, and maintaining a healthy work-life balance.

REPRODUCTIVE HEALTH:

Attend regular gynaecological check-ups, discuss family planning options, and stay informed about reproductive health.

SUN PROTECTION:

Protect the skin from harmful UV rays by using sunscreen, wearing protective clothing, and avoiding excessive sun exposure to prevent skin cancer.

QUIT SMOKING:

Smoking is a significant risk factor for various diseases. Quitting smoking has immediate and long-term health benefits.

LIMIT ALCOHOL INTAKE:

If consuming alcohol, do so in moderation. Excessive alcohol consumption can contribute to various health issues.

REGULAR EXERCISE:

Engage in regular physical activity to maintain a healthy weight, reduce stress, and improve overall well-being.

BREAST HEALTH AND BREAST CANCER AWARENESS

Breast health and breast cancer awareness are crucial for women's well-being. Here are key aspects to consider:

BREAST SELF-EXAMS:
Regular breast self-exams help women become familiar with their breasts and detect any changes. Perform these exams monthly.

CLINICAL BREAST EXAMS:
Include clinical breast exams as part of regular check-ups with healthcare providers. Professionals can identify abnormalities that may not be apparent during self-exams.

MAMMOGRAMS:
Mammograms are essential for early detection of breast cancer. Guidelines for when to start and how often to have mammograms may vary, so consult with a healthcare provider.

KNOW YOUR RISK:
Understand your personal risk factors for breast cancer, including family history, genetic factors, and lifestyle choices. This knowledge can inform screening and prevention strategies.

BREAST CANCER SCREENING GUIDELINES:
Stay informed about recommended breast cancer screening guidelines, which may include mammography, MRI, or other imaging techniques based on individual risk factors.

BREAST HEALTH EDUCATION:
Educate yourself about breast health and breast cancer. Knowledge empowers women to make informed decisions about their health.

HEALTHY LIFESTYLE CHOICES:
Adopt a healthy lifestyle, including regular exercise, a balanced diet, limited alcohol consumption, and not smoking. These factors contribute to overall well-being and may reduce the risk of breast cancer.

BREASTFEEDING:
If possible, consider breastfeeding. Research suggests that breastfeeding may have protective effects against breast cancer.

STAY ACTIVE:
Regular physical activity is associated with a lower risk of breast cancer. Aim for at least 150 minutes of moderate-intensity exercise per week.

CLINICAL BREAST EXAMS FOR YOUNGER WOMEN:
Younger women should also have regular clinical breast exams, especially if there is a family history of breast cancer or other risk factors.

GENETIC COUNSELING AND TESTING:
If there's a family history of breast cancer or known genetic mutations, consider genetic counselling and testing to assess your risk.

EARLY DETECTION SAVES LIVES:
Emphasize the importance of early detection. Regular screenings can identify breast cancer at an early, more treatable stage.

SUPPORT BREAST CANCER AWARENESS CAMPAIGNS:
Participate in and support breast cancer awareness campaigns. These efforts raise awareness, promote early detection, and fund research for better treatments.

GYNECOLOGICAL HEALTH

Gynaecological health is a vital aspect of overall well-being for women. Here are key considerations:

REGULAR CHECK-UPS:

Schedule regular gynaecological check-ups with a healthcare provider. These visits often include pelvic exams, Pap smears, and discussions about reproductive health.

PELVIC EXAMS:

Pelvic exams help assess the health of reproductive organs. They can detect abnormalities, infections, or other issues.

PAP SMEARS:

Pap smears are crucial for detecting cervical abnormalities early, reducing the risk of cervical cancer. Follow recommended screening guidelines based on age and risk factors.

STI SCREENINGS:

Regular screenings for sexually transmitted infections (STIs) are essential for sexual health. Early detection and treatment are key.

CONTRACEPTION:

Discuss contraceptive options with your healthcare provider to find a method that suits your lifestyle and reproductive goals.

MENSTRUAL HEALTH:

Monitor and track your menstrual cycle. Changes in menstrual patterns can indicate hormonal imbalances or other issues.

MENOPAUSE MANAGEMENT:

If approaching or experiencing menopause, discuss symptoms and management options with your healthcare provider.

BREAST HEALTH:

Include breast health assessments as part of routine check-ups Perform breast self-exams regularly, and discuss any concerns with you healthcare provider.

PELVIC FLOOR HEALTH:

Pelvic floor exercises can help maintain pelvic health and prevent issues such as incontinence.

REPRODUCTIVE HEALTH DISCUSSIONS:
Discuss family planning, fertility concerns, and reproductive health goals with your healthcare provider.

PREVENTIVE VACCINATIONS:
Stay up-to-date on vaccinations, including those for HPV, which can prevent cervical cancer.

BONE HEALTH:
Adequate calcium and vitamin D intake, along with weight-bearing exercises, contribute to strong bones and overall health.

ADDRESSING GYNECOLOGICAL CONCERNS:
If you experience any unusual symptoms, such as abnormal bleeding, pain, or discomfort, seek prompt medical attention.

MENTAL HEALTH AND WELL-BEING:
Gynaecological health is interconnected with mental well-being. Discuss any emotional or psychological concerns with your healthcare provider.

LIFESTYLE FACTORS:
Adopt a healthy lifestyle, including a balanced diet, regular exercise, sufficient sleep, and stress management.

PREVENTIVE SCREENINGS AND VACCINATIONS

Preventive screenings and vaccinations are essential components of women's healthcare. Here are some key screenings and vaccinations to consider:

SCREENINGS:

Pap Smear And Hpv Testing:

Regular Pap smears and HPV testing are crucial for cervical cancer screening. Follow recommended guidelines for frequency.

Mammograms:

Mammograms are vital for detecting breast cancer. Guidelines for when to start and how often to have mammograms may vary, so consult with a healthcare provider.

Colorectal Cancer Screening:

Depending on age and risk factors, women may need screenings such as colonoscopies or fecal occult blood tests to detect colorectal cancer.

Cholesterol And Blood Pressure Checks:

Regular checks for cholesterol levels and blood pressure help monitor cardiovascular health.

Bone Density Testing:

Women, especially postmenopausal, may need bone density testing to assess the risk of osteoporosis.

STI Screenings:

Regular screenings for sexually transmitted infections (STIs) are important for sexual health. Tests may include those for chlamydia, gonorrhoea, syphilis, and HIV.

Thyroid Function Tests:

Thyroid function tests help assess the health of the thyroid gland and hormonal balance.

Diabetes Screening:

Regular screenings for diabetes may include blood glucose tests to monitor blood sugar levels.

Skin Cancer Checks:
Regular skin examinations help detect any suspicious moles or skin changes that could indicate skin cancer.

Eye Exams:
Regular eye exams can detect vision issues, as well as conditions like glaucoma or age-related macular degeneration.

VACCINATIONS:

HPV Vaccine:
The HPV vaccine helps prevent human papillomavirus infections, reducing the risk of cervical and other cancers. It is recommended for both young girls and boys.

FLU Vaccine:
Annual flu vaccinations are recommended to protect against seasonal influenza.

TDAP and TD Vaccines:
Tdap vaccine (tetanus, diphtheria, and pertussis) is recommended during pregnancy. Td booster shots are given every 10 years.

HEPATITIS B Vaccine:
The hepatitis B vaccine helps prevent hepatitis B infections, which can lead to liver disease.

MMR Vaccine:
The MMR vaccine protects against measles, mumps, and rubella. It is essential for women planning pregnancy.

SHINGLES Vaccine:
The shingles vaccine is recommended for adults over a certain age to prevent shingles, a painful condition caused by the varicella-zoster virus.

PNEUMOCOCCAL Vaccine:
Pneumococcal vaccines help protect against pneumonia and other respiratory infections.

COVID-19 Vaccine:

As of my last knowledge update in January 2022, COVID-19 vaccination is recommended for eligible individuals to prevent severe illness and complications from the virus. Check for the latest recommendations.

WELLNESS AND LIFESTYLE

Maintaining wellness and adopting a healthy lifestyle are key priorities for women. Here are some aspects to consider:

BALANCED NUTRITION:
Prioritize a well-balanced diet rich in fruits, vegetables, whole grains, lean proteins, and healthy fats. Adequate nutrition is fundamental for overall health.

REGULAR EXERCISE:
Engage in regular physical activity, combining cardiovascular exercises, strength training, and flexibility exercises. Aim for at least 150 minutes of moderate-intensity exercise per week.

ADEQUATE HYDRATION:
Stay hydrated by drinking sufficient water throughout the day. Water is essential for various bodily functions and contributes to overall well-being.

SUFFICIENT SLEEP:
Aim for 7-9 hours of quality sleep each night. Establishing good sleep hygiene practices promotes physical and mental health.

STRESS MANAGEMENT:
Practice stress-reducing techniques such as meditation, deep breathing, yoga, or mindfulness to manage daily stressors effectively.

MENTAL HEALTH:
Prioritize mental health by seeking support when needed, fostering positive relationships, and taking time for activities that bring joy and relaxation.

REGULAR HEALTH CHECK-UPS:
Schedule regular check-ups with healthcare providers for preventive screenings, vaccinations, and overall health assessments.

AVOIDING HARMFUL SUBSTANCES:
Limit alcohol intake and avoid smoking and other harmful substances that can negatively impact health.

SUN PROTECTION:
Protect your skin from harmful UV rays by using sunscreen, wearing protective clothing, and avoiding excessive sun exposure.

SOCIAL CONNECTIONS:
Cultivate and maintain positive social connections. Strong social support is associated with better mental and physical well-being.

BREAST HEALTH AWARENESS:
Be proactive about breast health by performing regular breast self-exams, attending clinical breast exams, and following recommended mammogram guidelines.

REPRODUCTIVE HEALTH:
Stay informed about reproductive health, including family planning, contraceptive options, and regular gynecological check-ups.

BONE HEALTH:
Consume adequate calcium and vitamin D to support bone health. Weight-bearing exercises also contribute to strong bones.

CULTURAL AND PERSONAL VALUES:
Align wellness practices with personal and cultural values. Recognize the unique aspects of your identity and integrate them into your overall well-being.

CONTINUOUS LEARNING:
Stay curious and engaged in lifelong learning. This could include exploring new hobbies, taking courses, or staying informed about health-related topics.

HOLISTIC WELLNESS FOR WOMEN

Holistic wellness for women involves nurturing every aspect of their well-being—physical, mental, emotional, and spiritual. Here's a more in-depth look at each dimension:

PHYSICAL WELLNESS:

Nutrition: Prioritize a balanced diet with a variety of nutrient-dense foods.

Exercise: Engage in regular physical activity to promote cardiovascular health, strength, and flexibility.

Rest: Ensure sufficient and quality sleep to support overall physical health and recovery.

MENTAL WELLNESS:

Mindfulness And Meditation: Practice mindfulness and meditation to reduce stress, increase self-awareness, and enhance mental clarity.

Stress Management: Develop effective stress-coping mechanisms, such as deep breathing, yoga, or hobbies that bring joy.

Continuous Learning: Stimulate the mind through continuous learning and intellectual pursuits.

EMOTIONAL WELLNESS:

Self-Care: Prioritize self-care activities that bring joy and relaxation.

Express Emotions: Develop healthy ways to express and process emotions, whether through journaling, art, or open communication.

Positive Relationships: Cultivate and maintain positive relationships that provide support and emotional connection.

SOCIAL WELLNESS:

Social Connections: Foster a strong social support system by building and maintaining meaningful connections.

Community Engagement: Engage in community activities or volunteer work to contribute to a sense of purpose and belonging.

SPIRITUAL WELLNESS:

Mind-Body Practices: Explore mind-body practices, such as yog
or tai chi, to connect with your spiritual self.

Reflection And Meditation: Spend time in reflection an
meditation to explore personal values and beliefs.

Nature Connection: Connect with nature to nurture a sense of aw
and spiritual well-being.

REPRODUCTIVE AND SEXUAL WELLNESS:

Regular Check-Ups: Schedule regular gynaecological check-uµ
and screenings for reproductive health.

Safe Sex Practices: Practice safe sex and stay informed about sexu
health, including contraception and STI prevention.

ENVIRONMENTAL WELLNESS:

Sustainable Living: Make eco-friendly choices to suppoɪ
environmental well-being and contribute to a healthier planet.

Healthy Living Spaces: Create a positive and nurturing livir
environment.

FINANCIAL WELLNESS:

Budgeting: Manage finances responsibly through budgeting an
financial planning.

Financial Literacy: Stay informed about financial matters to mak
informed decisions about money and investments.

CULTURAL AND PERSONAL IDENTITY:

Embrace Diversity: Celebrate and embrace your cultural identit
and diversity.

Personal Values: Align wellness practices with personal values an
beliefs.

HOLISTIC HEALTH PRACTICES:
INTEGRATIVE MEDICINE:

Explore holistic health practices, such as acupuncture, herb
medicine, or aromatherapy, to complement traditional healthcare.

MIND-BODY PRACTICES

Mind-body practices can be incredibly beneficial for women, promoting holistic well-being by integrating mental, emotional, and physical aspects. Here are some mind-body practices tailored for women:

YOGA:

Yoga combines physical postures, breath control, and meditation. It enhances flexibility, strength, and mental focus while promoting relaxation.

MEDITATION:

Meditation involves cultivating mindfulness and focusing the mind to achieve a state of calm and clarity. It can reduce stress, improve emotional well-being, and enhance self-awareness.

TAI CHI:

Tai Chi is a gentle, flowing martial art that emphasizes slow, deliberate movements. It promotes balance, flexibility, and relaxation.

PILATES:

Pilates focuses on core strength, flexibility, and overall body awareness. It's an excellent practice for toning muscles and improving posture.

MINDFUL WALKING:

Walking mindfully involves paying attention to each step, breath, and the surrounding environment. It's a simple yet effective practice to enhance awareness and reduce stress.

BREATHWORK (PRANAYAMA):

Various breathwork techniques, such as deep diaphragmatic breathing or alternate nostril breathing, can calm the nervous system and improve respiratory health.

GUIDED IMAGERY:

Guided imagery involves creating vivid mental images to promote relaxation and reduce stress. It can be incorporated into meditation or relaxation exercises.

DANCE THERAPY:

Dance therapy combines movement and self-expression to enhance emotional well-being. It can be a fun and creative way to release tension and connect with emotions.

PROGRESSIVE MUSCLE RELAXATION (PMR):

PMR involves systematically tensing and relaxing different muscle groups to release physical tension and promote relaxation.

BIOFEEDBACK:

Biofeedback uses electronic monitoring to provide information about physiological processes. It helps individuals gain control over aspects like heart rate, muscle tension, and stress response.

AROMATHERAPY:

Aromatherapy involves using essential oils to enhance emotional and mental well-being. Scents like lavender, chamomile, and citrus can have calming effects.

JOURNALING:

Keeping a journal allows women to express thoughts and emotions, fostering self-reflection and promoting mental clarity.

ACUPUNCTURE:

Acupuncture involves the insertion of thin needles into specific points on the body to balance energy flow. It is used to alleviate stress, pain, and various health concerns.

MASSAGE THERAPY:

Massage not only relaxes muscles but also promotes mental well-being by reducing stress and enhancing the mind-body connection.

SOUND THERAPY:

Listening to calming sounds, such as nature sounds or gentle music, can have a soothing effect on the mind and nervous system.

These practices can be adapted to individual preferences and needs. Incorporating mind-body practices into daily routines can contribute to a sense of balance, reduce stress, and enhance overall well-being. If you're interested in exploring a specific practice or have questions, feel free to ask!

BALANCING WORK AND LIFE

Balancing work and life is a common challenge, and it's crucial for women to find harmony between professional and personal responsibilities. Here are some strategies to help achieve a better work-life balance:

SET CLEAR BOUNDARIES:
Clearly define work hours and non-work hours. Establishing boundaries helps prevent work from encroaching too much on personal time.

PRIORITIZE SELF-CARE:
Make self-care a priority. Schedule time for activities that rejuvenate you, whether it's exercise, reading, hobbies, or spending time with loved ones.

LEARN TO SAY NO:
Don't be afraid to say no when your plate is full. Prioritize tasks and commitments, and be realistic about what you can take on.

EFFECTIVE TIME MANAGEMENT:
Use time management techniques, such as creating to-do lists, prioritizing tasks, and setting realistic deadlines. This helps increase productivity and reduces stress.

ESTABLISH A SUPPORT SYSTEM:
Build a strong support system at work and at home. Communicate with your team about your needs, and seek help from family or friends when necessary.

FLEXIBLE WORK ARRANGEMENTS:
Explore flexible work options if available, such as remote work, flexible hours, or compressed workweeks. This can provide more control over your schedule.

DELEGATE RESPONSIBILITIES:

Delegate tasks at work and at home. Trusting others to take on certain responsibilities can lighten your load and create a more balanced life.

SET REALISTIC EXPECTATIONS:
Establish realistic expectations for yourself. Understand that it's okay not to be perfect and that some days may be more challenging than others.

CREATE RITUALS AND ROUTINES:
Establish daily or weekly rituals that help you transition between work and personal life. This can be a helpful signal for your mind to switch gears.

TECHNOLOGY BOUNDARIES:
Set boundaries with technology. Avoid checking work emails or messages during personal time, and consider turning off notifications.

INVEST IN PROFESSIONAL DEVELOPMENT:
Continuously invest in your professional development to enhance your skills. This can lead to increased efficiency at work and potentially more flexibility.

PLAN QUALITY FAMILY TIME:
Schedule dedicated quality time with family and loved ones. This reinforces the importance of personal relationships and helps maintain a strong support network.

TAKE BREAKS:
Schedule breaks during the workday to recharge. Short breaks can improve focus and prevent burnout.

REGULAR CHECK-INS:
Regularly assess your work-life balance and make adjustments as needed. Life is dynamic, and your priorities may evolve.

MINDFULNESS PRACTICES:
Incorporate mindfulness practices, such as meditation or deep breathing, to stay present and reduce stress.

Finding the right balance is a continuous process of adjustment. It about aligning your priorities, setting boundaries, and taking intention. steps to create a fulfilling and sustainable life. If you have specif questions or need further guidance, feel free to ask!

Milton Keynes UK
Ingram Content Group UK Ltd.
UKHW010631271123
433341UK00001B/144

9 798223 083771